Mwari, Chivanhu & Christianity

Gabriel James Dziya

Published by Gabriel James Dziya, 2023.

While every precaution has been taken in the preparation of this book, the publisher assumes no responsibility for errors or omissions, or for damages resulting from the use of the information contained herein.

MWARI, CHIVANHU & CHRISTIANITY

First edition. May 15, 2023.

ISBN: 979-8223986706

Written by Gabriel James Dziya.

Also by Gabriel James Dziya

Anthology Of Heavenly Visions
Demystifying The Anointing
Prophecies And Their Testimonies
Mwari, Chivanhu & Christianity

A Zimbabwean Perspective On Concepts Of Deity

Mwari, Chivanhu & Christianity

Gabriel James Dziya

Acknowledgement

I would like to express my deepest gratitude to all those who have contributed to the creation of this book on Mwari, Chivanhu, and Christianity.

First and foremost, I would like to thank my wife Rutendo Dziya for her unwavering support, encouragement, and inspiration throughout the entire writing process. Her love and dedication have been a constant source of strength and motivation.

I would also like to acknowledge the many spiritual guides who have been instrumental in shaping my understanding of these complex and sacred topics. Their wisdom and guidance have been numerous and precious, and I am deeply grateful for their insights and teachings.

Finally, I would like to express my appreciation to the countless individuals and communities who have shared their stories, experiences, and knowledge with me. Their generosity and openness have enriched this work and made it possible to explore these important themes with depth and compassion.

Thank you all for your contributions and support. May this book serve as a testament to the power of love, faith, and spiritual connection in our lives.

Preface

"Translation does not take place in a vacuum. Each translator is guided by a certain ideology or ideologies." – (Togarasei 1971, pp1)

For centuries, Chivanhu has been an integral part of Zimbabwean culture and spirituality. It is a belief system that is deeply rooted in the traditions and practices of the Shona people. However, the dominance of Christianity and Bible-based teachings have made it increasingly difficult to practice Chivanhu freely and openly in Zimbabwe. The clash between these two belief systems has led to a lot of misunderstandings and misconceptions about Chivanhu.

One of the main reasons for this is the mistranslation of Chivanhu. The Shona language is complex, and the translation of concepts and ideas can be challenging. As a result, many Chivanhu practices have been misunderstood and misrepresented by Christian missionaries and scholars who have attempted to translate them into English. This has led to a lot of confusion and misunderstanding between Christianity and Chivanhu.

The mistranslation of Chivanhu has also led to the demonisation of certain practices and beliefs. For example, practices such as ancestral veneration and *mabira* (a type of spiritual communion with the ancestral saints) have been labeled as demonic and evil by Christian missionaries and scholars. This has created a negative perception of Chivanhu practices among Zimbabweans who have been influenced by Christianity.

Despite these challenges, Chivanhu continues to thrive in Zimbabwe. Many Zimbabweans still practice Chivanhu despite the dominance of Christianity. However, there is a need for greater understanding and respect between these two belief systems. It is important to recognise that Chivanhu is an integral part of Zimbabwean culture and spirituality and should be respected as such.

This book explores the difficulties of practicing Chivanhu in Zimbabwe and the impact of Christianity on this indigenous belief system. It seeks to promote greater understanding and respect between these two belief systems and to highlight the importance of preserving and promoting Chivanhu as an integral part of Zimbabwean culture and spirituality.

Introduction

"Chivanhu religion is a testament to the resilience and creativity of African peoples, and it serves as an inspiration to all who seek to uphold the dignity and worth of every human being." (Chakrabarti, "The Universal Significance of Chivanhu Religion," 2017)

It is not possible to discuss anything concerning Chivanhu without first discussing the concept of Mudzimu. The word "Mudzimu" has been badly translated to mean "ancestral spirit". A better translation would be "ancestral saint". Mudzimu do not refer to the spirits of every person to have lived and died as it is clearly understood, according to Chivanhu theology, that only those who lived saintly, holy, righteous lives were glorified by the power of Mwari (God) and His Holy Spirit (Mudzimu waMwari).

It is through a life of intercession (kukumbirira) of behalf of the family and those in the community, moral excellence and good works that one's reputation is established in the sacred spiritual office of a "Svikiro" (one who works with mudzimu). Again, the word "Svikiro" itself is badly translated to "spirit medium".

The Western understanding of what a spirit medium is too broad and general. It invokes images of random communications with random dead people and spirits. With Chivanhu however, what we are looking at is a bonafide African take on Monotheism (the idea that there is one God who created the Universe).

It is a religion which has remarkably similar concepts to Judaism specifically. For example, as I alluded to earlier, Chivanhu theology has within it the doctrine of one God. Within it the doctrine the doctrine of the Holy Spirit of God (Mudzimu waMwari). The God of Chivanhu has a personal name, "Mwari", just the personal name of the God of Judaism is Yahweh (Jehovah is the German transliteration).

Chivanhu venerates its ancestral saints much like Judaism does in acknowledging and even praying to the God of the ancestral saints Abraham, Isaac and Jacob. They also maintain their own ancestral tribes (the 12 tribes of Israel) as we maintain our own tribes (marudzi nemitupo ose eZimbabwe).

As in Judaism Mwari has a common adjectival title, "Musikavanhu" (the creator of humanity). In Judaism we see adjectival titles such as "Almighty" for example.

The fact is, when you translate properly the religion of Chivanhu it is as close to an African translation of Judaism, this reality itself is profoundly fascinating.

Chivanhu has concepts of good and evil, righteousness and wickedness. There are "good guys" (working with Mudzimu in service to God's love for humanity) and "bad guys" (those working witchcraft and evil occult practices {kuromba}). Judaism, like Chivanhu extols righteousness and holy living. In Chivanhu, Mudzimu will depart from you if you are morally corrupt.

The moral commandments of Chivanhu and Judaism are virtually identical. For instance, the famous "Ten Commandments" from the Bible are also commandments within Chivanhu for those practicing by the Spirit of God in righteousness and true holiness.

Unfortunately, those who practice the occult, without the use of Mudzimu have used the general ignorance of the public and branded themselves as Chivanhu practitioners. These notorious individuals tend to find themselves in the news cycles more than the genuine practitioners of Chivanhu. As such the collective subconscious awareness of the general public associates Chivanhu with that which bizarre, immoral, backward and even evil.

For those who have had the endurance to pay close attention and look beneath the superficial surface of popular culture, there remains a divine reality and true connection with our beloved Mwari and this connection is mediated by the blessed work of Mudzimu.

Can true divinity and genuine connection with God come from Africa? If you find yourself unable to answer "yes", then you will find this book a tough pill to swallow. If you are able to see life and this world from a bird's eye view, the obviousness of the truth is immediately clear to you. God has manifested Himself to different people, cultures and races across time and black Africans are not the exception to this and in Zimbabwe we have a profound, intelligent, dignified, holy expression of this.

There remains some work for us to do in order to express boldly what is true and dismiss what is myth, superstition, lies and propaganda. If Chivanhu is to be rejected by some of the world let it be rejected on its own merits (or lack thereof). What is a crime against humanity is the rejection of Chivanhu due to a misrepresentation of what is actually happening within the religion.

In order for these discussions to be open to people from all walks of life and even our brothers and sisters from the international community it is presented here in English.

Mudzimu

"Chivanhu religion represents the wisdom and knowledge of our ancestors, and it serves as a bridge between the past, present, and future." (Mugabe, "The Significance of Chivanhu Religion in African Society," 2014)

Defining Mudzimu

Part of the major problem in interpreting the Chivanhu tradition comes from a shallow, overly simplified idea of what Chivanhu means when it speak of "mudzimu". Which is roughly translated in English "ancestral spirits".

Ancestral saints are specifically people directly related to you by blood. That is the ancestral part. There is nothing inherently evil about ancestries in itself as even the Christian Bible goes to great lengths to show and preserve ancestral geneologies. I prefer the term "saints" to spirits, because the word "saint" has within it, the necessary understanding that Mudzimu are righteous, holy and connected to God (Mwari) and his Holy Spirit (Mudzimu waMwari). To miss the saintly aspect of Mudzimu is to misunderstand the spiritual reality of what these blessed beings are and how best they can impact the life of a Chivanhu practioner.

It is through their saintly connection to God that Mudzimu have power which has the ability to affect possitive change to those who are on the truth path of a spiritual seeker by the Holy Spirit of God. To omit the saintly nature of Mudzimu is to rob the word of much of its sacred inherent meaning. They become just like any other spirits of the dead of which Chivanhu theology has different words for general spirits of the dead ranging from *zvipoko* (ghosts), *ngozi* (poltergists), *madzinza* (ancestral spirits of those who practiced evil). In Shona, no one would mistake a ghost (the spirit of a dead person with no connection to God) and Mudzimu.

Thus, we can say with conviction and clarity: **Mudzimu is an ancestral saint sent by Mwari to assist His people on their path to spiritual enlightenment in holiness by the power of the Holy Spirit.**

Speaking to the general dead is not something Chivanhu does directly unless it is for the purpose of performing spiritual cleansing to lay to rest the spirits of the dead. Just as Christianity has a concept of Gods adversary "Satan" who is "the accuser of the brethren", that is to say, "the accuser of God's people". Similarly, Chivanhu too has a concept of Gods people being harassed by witches (varoyi) and wizards (vakaromba).

Chivanhu may not directly use the term "Satan" but it is understood that witches and wizards do not get their power from God but they serve other dark entities. Musikavanhu does not condone witchcraft. For example, in Chivanhu if the medium begins to perform dark magic the ancestral saint (Mudzimu) departs from that person and cannot work with him anymore.

What it means is that in Chivanhu theology there is a concept of Gods people and people that are on the side of evil. That is a peculiarly "Abrahamic" concept. The Abrahamic religions (Judaism, Christianity and Islam) view a difference between Gods people and "the unrighteous" so to speak. As it so happens Chivanhu is the same way.

The term Mudzimu refers to the living spirits of righteous holy people and that died whilst possessing an expanded consciousness of God's Spirit (Mudzimu waMwari). These people have a certain "aliveness" due to their connection to God, the source of all life. Their bodies are dead but their spirits are alive in God. Mudzimu correspond to saints in the Bible. The Bible makes a distinction between how it refers to "the dead" versus how it refers to saints. Those who die in the Lord are never said to be "dead" but rather asleep (eg Act 7:60) or alive in "Abraham's bosom:

Nyikadzimu and Abraham's bosom

Luke 16:23 And being in torments in Hades, he lifted up his eyes and saw Abraham afar off, and Lazarus in his bosom.

Here Jesus tells a story that the scriptures do not refer to as "a parable". It the story which shows two states of the dead. One state is a state of torment that is the state of dying without a connection to God. The other state is a state of saintly connection to God in the presence of the most ancient ancestor of the Jews.

In Chivanhu too, there is a difference between the place of the ancestors in the spirit realm and the place of the general dead. The Heavenly realm of Chivanhu, which corresponds with Abraham's bosom is called, "Nyikadzimu". This can be roughly translated to, "the land of the saints". This is the Chivanhu version of Heaven where adherents of Chivanhu long to go to join the noblest members of their tribe.

It is not every human being that dies that becomes a Mudzimu. To think that is to miss the whole idea completely. Only those who died while having a strong connection to God and through His Spirit become Mudzimu (saints).

When Mudzimu comes it is not just any random dead person from your family. It is the spirit of an excellent godly saint. That is the theology of Chivanhu and the right understanding of how the religion works if you ask the spiritually mature.

Jesus Speaks To Ancestral Saints

Notice also that Jesus Himself spoke to saints who were spirits when he was on the famous "Mount of Transfiguration":

Matthew 17:1 Now after six days Jesus took Peter, James, and John his brother, led them up on a high mountain by themselves;

2 and He was transfigured before them. His face shone like the sun, and His clothes became as white as the light.

3 And behold, Moses and Elijah appeared to them, talking with Him.

There may be some debate as to whether Elijah is alive or not, I am willing to allow that. Yet, Moses died (Deuteronomy 34:5). And here we find Jesus talking to Moses. Communication with the dead is prohibited (Deuteronomy 18:10-12). If Jesus violated the law of God by talking to Moses then He ceases to be sinless.

No one sees this as sin because instinctively the people realise that there is a distinct difference between any old dead person and being the spirit of a saint who is in God. If this was not so then Jesus sinned right there in that mountain. This cannot be, because no one reading the early gospel accounts seemed to have a problem with Jesus doing this. In spiritual theology it is dishonest to not acknowledge even as a Christian that there is a difference between general spirits of the dead (ghosts) and the spirits of saints.

Furthermore, these saints are particularly of the bloodline of the Jewish people of whom Jesus was a part of. Moses and Elijah are saints from the Jewish ancestry just here we have Ambuya Nehanda and Kaguvi who are saints from the Zimbabwean ancestry.

Melchizedek Was A Saint That Did Not Share Abrahamic Ancestry. There is no good reason to dismiss the ideas that a saint can be the spirit of a black man or black woman. I must assert that a black African man or woman can be a saint of God. Did we not have our own versions of Melchizedek here in Africa? Our version of the saints are Mudzimu, and that is the proper understanding of that aspect of our spiritual connection to God.

Melchizedek was not of Abrahamic decent and yet he had a connection with God that was strong enough to bless even Abraham. He was of a different nation, culture and he even called God by a different name to that which Abraham used a different name for God, referring to Him as "El Elyon" (Genesis 14:19 – God Most High) which Abraham himself never used. Abraham also never used the Shona name for God (Mwari) yet Mwari remains a divine name and expression of God in the same way El Elyon is.

A Comparison Between Mudzimu And Bible Saints

The Chivanhu religion, like many other religions, has its own unique terminology and concepts that are difficult to translate into other languages, including English. One such concept is the word "Mudzimu," which is used to describe the spirits of ancestors who are believed to have a spiritual presence in the lives of their descendants. While there is no direct equivalent to the term "Mudzimu" in the Bible, the concept of "saints" comes closest in terms of its meaning and significance.

The term "saint" is used throughout the Bible to describe those who are set apart for God's service and who exhibit moral and ethical purity. In the Hebrew Bible, the term "saint" is translated from the Hebrew word "qadosh," which means "holy" or "set apart." In the New Testament, the term "saint" is translated from the Greek word "hagios," which also means "holy" or "set apart."

The idea of holiness is central to the concept of "Mudzimu" in the Chivanhu religion. In Shona, the term for this aspect of holiness is "kuyera," which refers to a state of moral and ethical purity that only the righteous can attain. The attributes and character of Mudzimu are similar to those of the saints in the Bible, as they are believed to have divine power and the ability to intercede on behalf of their descendants.

In the Bible, the saints are also believed to have a spiritual presence in the lives of believers. In Hebrews 12:1, the writer speaks of "a great cloud of witnesses" who surround us. This cloud of witnesses refers to the saints who have gone before us and who continue to inspire and encourage us in our faith. Similarly, in the Chivanhu religion, the spirits of ancestors are believed to be present and active in the lives of their descendants.

While the term "saint" may not capture the full meaning and significance of the term "Mudzimu," it comes closest in terms of its meaning and function. The concept of holiness and spiritual presence is central to both the saints in the Bible and the spirits of ancestors in the Chivanhu religion. Both serve as examples and intercessors for those who seek to live a life of moral and ethical purity.

Spiritual Cleansing Required When Receiving Mudzimu

When someone receives Mudzimu, they must undergo a radical cleansing period and to be in impeccable moral and holiness standing before they can flow in the fulness of their gifting. According to Chivanhu theology, one does not inherit weaknesses from Mudzimu but they come from what are called "Madzinza" roughly translated "generational curses".

This is the first major issue one must be cleansed from in order to flow freely in the Spirit of God. This cleansing work is best performed by by someone who is already a mature cleansed medium themselves. It is possible to receive cleansing from generational curses through one's own prayers and faith alone, but some cases require some outside support from another spiritual person.

The other major area from which one needs cleansing is from witchcraft attacks. Witches and wizards with deep occult knowledge can render most of your gifts ineffective if they use sufficient effort. One can be cleansed of these things by a medium that is well connected to God.

In Chivanhu theology, there are certain evil spirits known as *"Madzinza"* that can mimic Mudzimu. These spirits arise from Madzinza and witchcraft attacks. Most of what has been negatively attributed to Mudzimu, is a manifestation of these Madzinza. It takes one with keenness of perception to separate true saintly Mudzimu, from evil malicious Madzinza. These evil spirits are to be cast out under the unction of the Spirit of God by a medium that is holy and free from such things.

The concept of Mudzimu is a fundamental aspect of Chivanhu religion, which is practiced by many Zimbabwean communities. The term Mudzimu refers to ancestral saints who have the power to intercede on behalf of the living and to provide guidance and protection. The importance of Mudzimu in Chivanhu religion is reflected in the various rituals, ceremonies, and practices that are designed to honour and appease these ancestral saints. In this analysis, I explore the significance of Mudzimu in Chivanhu religion and argue that they are best understood as righteous and holy figures, rather than simply as ancestral spirits.

The concept of Mudzimu is deeply rooted in the belief that the spirits of the ancestors continue to exist and play a role in the lives of the living. According to Chivanhu tradition, when a person dies, their spirit does not vanish but rather continues to exist in the spiritual realm. The ancestors are believed to have the power to influence the lives of their descendants, and they are regarded as sources of wisdom, guidance, and protection. The belief in Mudzimu is therefore an important aspect of the connection between the living and the dead, and it serves to reinforce the social and cultural ties that bind Zimbabwean communities together.

While the term "ancestral spirits" is often used to describe Mudzimu, this translation is inadequate in capturing the full significance of these figures. Mudzimu are not simply disembodied entities that exist in the spiritual realm; they are believed to be righteous and holy figures who have attained a special status in the afterlife. As such, they are closer to the concept of what a saint is in other religious traditions. Mudzimu are revered for their wisdom, their moral character, and their ability to intercede on behalf of the living. They are not viewed as malevolent or harmful entities, but rather as benevolent and protective figures who are concerned with the well-being of their descendants.

The importance of Mudzimu in Chivanhu religion is reflected in the various rituals and practices that are designed to honour and appease these Ancestral Saints. For example, the ceremony of *kurova guva* is a ritual that is performed to ensure that the spirits of the ancestors are properly appeased and that they will continue to provide guidance and protection to their descendants. Similarly, the practice of *nhimbe* involves the offering of food, drink, and other goods to the ancestors as a sign of respect and gratitude.

Conclusion On Mudzimu Translation

The concept of Mudzimu is a fundamental aspect of Chivanhu religion, and it reflects the belief that the spirits of the ancestors continue to play a role in the lives of the living. While the term "ancestral spirits" is often used to describe these figures, it is more appropriate to view them as ancestral saints who are revered for their wisdom, moral character, and ability to intercede on behalf of the living. The importance of Mudzimu in Chivanhu religion is reflected in the various rituals and practices that are designed to honor and appease these figures, and they serve to reinforce the social and cultural ties that bind Zimbabwean communities together.

Mwari Musikavanhu - A Unique

20

Concept of Deity

"Chivanhu religion is a manifestation of the divine presence in our lives, and it helps us to connect with our spiritual selves and with the world around us." (Mafukidze, "The Sacredness of Chivanhu Religion," 2015)

The term Mwari is derived from the Shona word "Mwari" which means "He who is." This noun is often used to describe the Supreme Being or God in Chivanhu beliefs. It is a term that is similar to the Hebrew noun Yahweh (I am that I am), which is used to describe God in the Bible. In essence it is as close to a one to one translation as you could hope for from one language to another.

One of the unique aspects of Mwari as a deity is that he is not visually described. Instead, he is conceptualised through various titles that describe his attributes and characteristics. These titles include "Mwari Musikavanhu," which means "God the Creator of humanity", "Mwari Mweya," which means "God the Holy Spirit," and "Mwari Muponesi," which means "God the Savior."

In Chivanhu beliefs, human beings are seen as a part of nature, and they interact with both nature and spirits. The doctrine of the Holy Spirit is also central to Chivanhu beliefs. The Holy Spirit is seen as a powerful force that gives life to all things and is responsible for the movement and energy of the universe.

Mwari is also seen as a loving and just God who is guided by the righteous holy ethics of Chivanhu. These ethics include the importance of respect for all living things, the need for harmony and balance between human beings and nature, and the importance of social responsibility and community involvement.

One of the key aspects of Mwari as a deity is his role as a provider and protector. In Chivanhu beliefs, Mwari is seen as the source of all life and the provider of all things. He is also seen as a protector who watches over his people and guides them through difficult times.

However, Mwari is also seen as a just God who punishes those who act against his righteous holy ethics. In Chivanhu beliefs, this punishment can take the form of illness, misfortune, or other forms of suffering.

Overall, Mwari Musikavanhu is a unique concept of deity that is central to Chivanhu beliefs and practices. It is a concept that emphasizes the importance of respect for all living things, the need for harmony and balance between human beings and nature, and the importance of social responsibility and community involvement. Mwari is seen as a loving and just God who is guided by the righteous holy ethics of Chivanhu, and he is conceptualized through various titles that describe his attributes and characteristics.

The Emergence Of Chivanhu

The Shona people are one of the largest ethnic groups in Zimbabwe, with a population of over 10 million. They are believed to have migrated to the region from the north and central Africa around the 10th century CE, and developed a complex society and culture over the centuries that followed.

There is strong evidence to suggest that the Shona people occupying Great Zimbabwe were actively engaged in international trade with people who spoke different languages.

One key piece of evidence is the presence of foreign artifacts in Great Zimbabwe, including pottery, glass beads, and other luxury items. According to a 2011 article in the Journal of African History by Innocent Pikirayi, "the presence of imported items, such as Chinese celadon, Arabian glass, and Indian beads, indicates that Great Zimbabwe was a center of long-distance trade and commerce." Pikirayi notes that these artifacts likely came from trade networks that extended as far as the Indian Ocean and the Swahili coast.

Another important piece of evidence is the discovery of Shona artifacts in other parts of Africa. According to a 2010 article in the Journal of Social Archaeology by Matthew Curtis, "archaeological evidence from sites in Zambia and Mozambique suggests that the Shona engaged in long-distance trade and cultural exchange with neighboring societies." This indicates that the Shona were active participants in regional trade networks, and were not isolated or self-sufficient.

Additionally, historical accounts from Arab and Portuguese traders provide further evidence of the Shona's participation in international trade. As noted in a 2018 article in the Journal of Southern African Studies by Innocent Chirisa and Josephine Nhongo-Simbanegavi, "Arab and Portuguese accounts from the 16th and 17th centuries describe the Shona people as skilled traders and craftspeople who were highly valued for their knowledge of mining, metalworking, and agriculture." These accounts describe the exchange of gold, ivory, and other goods between the Shona and traders from as far away as India and China.

This evidence shows that the Shona were not a savage, primitive, illiterate people as colonialist propaganda suggested. The presence of foreign artifacts at Great Zimbabwe and the discovery of Shona artifacts in other parts of Africa demonstrate that the Shona were active participants in regional and international trade networks. Furthermore, the historical accounts from Arab and Portuguese traders provide evidence of the Shona's knowledge and expertise in various fields. As Pikirayi notes, "the presence of imported goods and the evidence of sophisticated mining and metalworking techniques indicate that Great Zimbabwe was a significant player in the regional economy." This evidence challenges the Eurocentric view that African societies were isolated and inferior, and instead suggests that they were active participants in global trade and commerce.

There is evidence to suggest that the Shona people were engaged in international trade and cultural exchange as early as the 11th century CE, as evidenced by the archaeological remains of Great Zimbabwe. According to UNESCO, Great Zimbabwe "represents the most significant and impressive architectural achievement of southern Africa's Late Iron Age civilization" (UNESCO). The city was a center of trade and culture, with evidence of trade connections to the East African coast, the Middle East, and even China.

The sophisticated religious beliefs and practices of the Shona people and the Chivanhu religion are comparable to other popular religions in their complexity and sophistication. Like many other religions, Chivanhu emphasizes the importance of living a moral and ethical life, treating others with kindness and compassion, and striving to align one's actions with the divine will.

In terms of chronology, the Shona people have a long and rich history that spans over a millennium. They developed a complex society and culture over this time, with a rich tradition of art, music, and literature. The emergence of Chivanhu as a modern religion reflects the ongoing cultural and historical evolution of the Shona people, and their continued engagement with modern ideologies and global trends.

The Zimbabwean Interpretation Of Christ And Mwari

"Chivanhu religion is a living tradition that adapts to changing circumstances while remaining true to its core principles and values." (Makoni, "The Evolution of Chivanhu Religion in Zimbabwe," 2019)

According to the 2021 World Religious Freedom Report, approximately 40% of Zimbabweans adhere to African initiated churches. That is the highest number by far of any religious group in the country. As we can compare other figures from the same report:
- Christianity (other than African initiated churches): 30%
- Islam: 1%
- Hinduism: less than 1%
- Judaism: less than 1%
- Other religions: less than 1%
- No religion/atheism: 20%
- Unspecified/unknown: 8%

Regarding Chivanhu, it is a traditional religion that is practiced by some Zimbabweans. However, the World Religious Freedom Report does not provide specific data on the percentage of Zimbabweans who adhere to Chivanhu. Having said that, the increase in African Initiated Church adherents does point to an increase in Chivanhu indirectly as some African initiated Churches allow for and even directly practice varying degrees of Chivanhu, for example:

Johan Masowe weChishanu Mudzimu unoyera

Johan Masowe weChishanu venguwo tsvuku

Johan Masowe weChishanu yeNyenyedzi nomwe

Mugodhi Apostolic Faith Church

Jekenishini Church

Zion Christian Church

This is not an exhaustive list by any means and each denomination does have different nuances as to what extent Chivanhu is embraced or in other cases, tolerated.

Add the fact that Protestant and Catholic Christians also frequent these AIC unofficially and you are soon confronted with a reality that many Zimbabwean Christians are encountering Chivanhu directly or indirectly. It behooves us to have intelligent spiritual conversations around the reasons why this happening en masse.

In many of these churches, the practice of Chivanhu is seen as a way of incorporating traditional African spirituality and culture into Christian worship. For example, in the Mugodhi Apostolic Faith Mission, Chivanhu is seen as a way of incorporating ancestral veneration into Christian worship, while in the Zion Christian Church, Chivanhu is seen as a way of emphasizing the importance of African culture and traditions.

It must be made clear that veneration is by no means a form of worship. Under the Chivanhu system it is Mwari who reigns supreme as God Almighty (Mwari Samasimba) that is the one and only object of worship. All the Ancestral Saints (Midzimu) and various Ministering Spirits (Mashavi) are in service to the ultimate worship of Mwari Musikavanhu. It is true monotheism in all its glory and at this point we should we should all take a collective deep breath and take a profound pause to just accept that.

The practice of syncretism between Christianity and Chivanhu is on the rise in Zimbabwe for several reasons. First, many Zimbabweans feel that Christianity alone does not fully represent their cultural identity and spiritual beliefs. Incorporating Chivanhu into Christian worship can provide a sense of cultural continuity and connection to their ancestral traditions.

Second, the practice of Chivanhu is seen by some as a way of addressing social and economic challenges in Zimbabwe. Many Zimbabweans face poverty, unemployment, and political instability, and some believe that the practice of Chivanhu can provide spiritual and emotional support during difficult times.

Finally, the rise of syncretism between Christianity and Chivanhu also reflects a broader trend of cultural and religious pluralism in Zimbabwe and other parts of sub-Saharan Africa. As people become more connected to global networks and exposed to new ideas and beliefs, they may seek to create new forms of religious expression that reflect local cultural and spiritual traditions.

Is this really the same God at work here or are we missing something vital? I will share more on my perspective on the doctrine of God (Mwari) and what the most reasonable perspective to prefer is.

The Significance Of The Name "Yahweh"

The name Yahweh holds great significance in the Bible and is one of the most important names for God in the Hebrew Scriptures. Yahweh is the personal name of the God of Israel and is often translated as "I am who I am" or "I will be who I will be" (Exod. 3:14). This name was considered so sacred by the ancient Hebrews that they would not even pronounce it aloud. Instead, they would use the title Adonai, meaning "Lord," when speaking of Yahweh.

The significance of the name Yahweh can be seen in its use throughout the Hebrew Scriptures. It is used over 6,800 times in the Old Testament alone, demonstrating its importance to the Israelites. The name Yahweh is often associated with God's covenant relationship with Israel, and it is used in many places to emphasize God's faithfulness and steadfast love for His people (Deut. 7:9; Isa. 54:10).

The name God is often used as a generic term for a deity, but it falls short in capturing the personal and relational nature of Yahweh. The name God can refer to any god or gods, whereas Yahweh is the personal name of the God of Israel. In the New Testament, the name Yahweh is often replaced with the Greek word Kurios, meaning "Lord," to emphasize the lordship of Jesus Christ (Rom. 10:9).

It is important to note that the name Yahweh cannot be simply substituted for the name of another deity like Mwari from the Chivanhu religion. The name Yahweh is uniquely tied to the history, culture, and theology of the Hebrew people, and it cannot be divorced from its context without losing its meaning and significance. Similarly, the name Mwari holds great significance and meaning within the Chivanhu religion and cannot be substituted for the name Yahweh without losing its cultural and theological context.

In conclusion, the name Yahweh is a highly significant and personal name for the God of Israel in the Hebrew Scriptures. It emphasizes God's covenant relationship with His people and His faithfulness and steadfast love towards them. While the name God is often used as a generic term for a deity, it falls short in capturing the personal and relational nature of Yahweh. It is important to respect the cultural and theological context in which these names hold significance and not substitute one for the other without understanding their full meaning and significance.

The Conflation of Mwari with Yahweh

Mwari and Yahweh are two distinct perspectives on monotheistic deity from two different religious systems that developed in different geographical areas. Mwari is the Supreme Being in Chivanhu beliefs, while Yahweh is the God of Judaism. However, over time, these two deities have become conflated into one, due to various factors such as translation and cultural contact.

One of the main factors that led to the conflation of Mwari with Yahweh is the translation of the personal noun Yahweh with the personal noun Mwari. When Christian missionaries came to Zimbabwe and began translating Chivanhu texts into English, they often used the general noun "God" to refer to Mwari. This led to a conflation of Mwari with the God of Christianity, who is seen as the same God as the God of Judaism.

Another factor that contributed to the conflation of Mwari with Yahweh is the similarities between Chivanhu and Judaism. There are four key similarities between these two belief systems that made the conflation of Mwari with Yahweh possible:

1. Monotheism: Both Chivanhu and Judaism are monotheistic religions, which means they believe in only one God.

2. Ancestral Veneration: Both Chivanhu and Judaism place a strong emphasis on ancestral veneration (veneration is not worship). In Chivanhu beliefs, ancestors are seen as intermediaries between the living and Mwari, while in Judaism, ancestors are revered and honoured in a similar way.

3. Ethics: Both Chivanhu and Judaism have a strong emphasis on ethical behavior. The righteous holy ethics of Chivanhu emphasize the importance of respect for all living things, the need for harmony and balance between human beings and nature, and the importance of social responsibility and community involvement. Similarly, Judaism emphasizes ethical behavior, including the Ten Commandments.

4. Creation: Both Chivanhu and Judaism have creation stories that emphasize the importance of God as the creator of all things.

These similarities made it possible for Christian missionaries and scholars to conflate Mwari with Yahweh, as they saw similarities between the two deities and their respective belief systems.

However, it is important to note that while there may be similarities between Chivanhu and Judaism, they are two distinct belief systems with their own unique histories and practices. The conflation of Mwari with Yahweh has led to misunderstandings and misrepresentations of Chivanhu beliefs and practices, and it is important to recognise and respect the distinct nature of these two belief systems.

Etymology of God

Religion is the human interpretation of the idea of deity. Deity refers to the concept of God. If we look at the etymology of the word "god" we will not find anything particularly useful for us now. The word god is derived from the Lombardic word "Godin" which is a translation of the father of the Norse pantheon of gods - "Odin". Today when we think of the word God very few people associated with ancient Norse mythology and religion. In this case the derivation does not really have serious consequence for the most part. We all just kinda get what you are talking about when you say "God" right?

In practice today, the word "God" has nothing to do with the origins of the word. It now mostly means the one true creator and source of both spiritual and physical life. Now that means different things to different people depending on what religious or cultural lens they are using to conceptualise the idea of deity. Religions, like cultures, evolve over time and from generation to generation. For example, the Christianity that existed and was practiced worldwide just 100 years ago was different from what is being practiced today. And in fact if you go back in 100 year intervals for 2000 years you will see distinctly different ideas and practices as human beings continue to collectively grapple with the infinite idea of deity.

The Zimbabwean Interpretation Of God And Christianity

It is somewhat disconcerting to note that the Zimbabwean concepts, ideas and profound interpretation of this global ongoing negotiation on the idea of God and Christ is being largely ignored and labelled as nothing more ridiculous, backward cults. I reluctantly must use the misnomer given as they are referred to as "African Initiated Churches" (AIC). I confess I am a little amused at the "not so subtle" innuendo in that title. The word "initiated" itself when used in a religious context has connotations of occult, ritualistic, primitive practices and that which is "other" from the sacred Church of Jesus Christ.

There is stigma around AIC. Obviously. How could there not be? The Western interpretation of the Middle Eastern, Jewish Christ, it is called "church planting". When the African man brings his African interpretation of the Jewish Christ, it is called "initiating". Why the difference? Sadly, there is an odour of rubbishing that which is African even when it comes to the Church of Jesus Christ.

I can assure you that Paul and Peter did not wear a tie and suit nor did they have church buildings with pews and pulpits. These are merely Western interpretations of a religion. They are superficial things that should not obstruct us from the true purpose and reason for the meeting, which is the fact that Jesus is risen from the dead.

When Africans meet because Jesus is risen from the dead, an inordinate amount of attention is paid by outsiders to outward things such how they dress and sing in a distinctly African way. With focused attention if you look beyond this you will realise that the Holy Spirit is doing a profound work in Zimbabwe through various AIC.

It is not all sunshine and roses though. There is tremendous fracturing and denominationalism within the various AIC in Zimbabwe and I am sure many are disgruntled being just packed in the same lump like that. Be that as it may, from a birds eye view let us at leat celebrate that God is at work in Zimbabwe through Africans in a truly novel way.

In my estimation the denominationalism is something inherent in the Church of Jesus Christ even from the times of the Bible. In 1 Corinthians 3:3-4, the Apostle Paul describes the cause of divisions as coming from the carnal nature of human beings. According to wikipedia there are over 22 000 recognised protestant Churches (every Western style Church that is not Roman Catholic is protestant). The division in AIC doctrines and practices should not overly alarm us given this reality that exists in the Church worldwide.

Broadly speaking there are two types of AIC: those who allow for the practice of Chivanhu (to varying extents) and those who do not (officially) allow the practice of any Chivanhu for any reason. Chivanhu is the traditional monotheistic religion of the Shona Zimbabwean people that is practiced through the mediation of ancestral saints under the unction of the Holy Spirit. It is from this religion that we get the name of the Shona deity, "Mwari".

I had to pause for a moment there because, on one hand I opened by saying the derivation of the word "God" is basically trivial and of no real world consequences today for the most part. It is a word that despite its origins it has forever obtained its own meaning. It is not so with the word Mwari though. You cannot just do a one is to one translation with this word and expect there to be no consequences.

You see the noun "Mwari" is given in relation to a very specific, very powerful, very potent religion that was consecrated within the blood of very powerful spiritual Bantu people who existed centuries ago. It was consecrated by faith in Mwari under the power of the Holy Spirit, through the blood of various totem animals in the beginning and is now being presently sustained actively by various spiritual practitioners all over the country in the name of Mwari.

One or two people may protest too much and say He is called "Musikavanhu". And to those people I simply say that Musikavanhu is not a noun (personal name) it is an adjective roughly meaning "Creator of Mankind". The gramma rules for Shona are such that using an adjectival title rather than a proper noun is more reverential when referring to one such as God but, to be sure, His proper name is actually Mwari. To put this in perspective the proper name of the God of the Bible is Yahweh and a common adjective for Him is "Almighty".

The Shona people actually have absolutely no trouble pronouncing the word "Yahweh". Given this why then did the Colonial era missionaries opt to use the proper name of another deity in their Bible translations? Let us keep in mind that Chivanhu is actually a more modern religion than Christianity and at some point it was so successful that all the Shona peoples practiced it without exception. This means that colonists arrived to a situation where people already had a deep knowledge, connection and active practice to communicate with Mwari Musikavanhu (God the creator).

This was no half-baked effort or religion by any stretch of the imagination. Chivanhu theology is actually very deep and surprisingly similar to Judaism. For example Chivanhu independently teaches and conceptualises the Holy Spirit of God (Mudzimu waMwari).

Chivanhu identifies different types of spiritual beings such as angels (ngirozi) independently from the Christian Bible. Chivanhu teaches the concept of holiness (kuyera) in a very similar way to Judaism where it is something that is imparted by God directly, or by one of His holy beings or it can be achieved through moral excellence and purity.

The moral commandments in Chivanhu are very similar to Judaism for example the Ten Commandments are also commandments in Chivanhu without a single contradiction. Practitioners of Chivanhu are (were) also spiritually gifted moving in healing, casting out evil spirits, prophecy and have been speaking in tongues for centuries even before the famous Azuza street revival ("initiated" by the African American man - William J. Syemor in an African Methodist episcopal Church building at 312 Azuza street) spawned the Pentecostal/Charismatic movement (1906-1909).

All of this (Chivanhu) was happening in an organised way on a national level. For the missionaries to take the name of that God and use it in their Bible was a deliberate calculated attempt to use a subtle deception to help spread Christianity. Missionary trips to Zimbabwe that attempted to introduce the name "Jehovah" (the German transliteration of Yahweh) rather than the name "Mwari" all failed. It was easier to just use the name of the Shona people's own deity and say that they represented Mwari.

This was deliberate misinformation. The Bible makes a very big deal about "the name of the Lord (Yahweh)" and a Bible translator is no novice. They would have been very well aware of just the sacrilege of taking the name of the God of a whole other religion and printing that in the Bible as the name of God. We see then a conflation of two spiritual realities in the Shona translation of the Bible.

Christianity and Chivanhu in Zimbabwe have become joined at the hip for better of for worse for anytime you call the name "Mwari" you are calling on the name of the God of Chivanhu, albeit you likely are using the name of Jesus (whose true Hebrew name is Yeshua, which again, Shona people can pronounce just fine) to mediate this prayer. We see then within one prayer the name of a Chivanhu deity and the name of a Christian deity. This is what I refer to as the conflation of two religious concepts in a unique way.

It resulted in the conflation of two religions into one religion. One consequence of that is, when a Christian believer calls the name "Mwari" with absolute faith and deep emotional involvement, who are they really calling? Yahweh or Mwari? It seems very obvious when I put it that way but that is not what Christians are thinking when they call Mwari. Nevertheless, the latent Chivanhu in one's blood can inadvertently be activated if they call upon Mwari with sufficient intention. This has happened to many Christians unknowingly. When it happens in this way Chivanhu becomes active in the believers body and they may begin to interact with different types of spirit beings that are related to the Chivanhu religion.

Blind Speculation And Archaic Spiritual Superstition Is Sadly Rampant In Zimbabwe

Without proper guidance and teaching about these things Christian pastors have turned to blind speculation and simply making up answers to things they do not understand well enough. It is shocking to me that in Western style Charismatic Christianity no distinction is made between mermaids (manjuzu) and marine spirits (mbereka). The distinction in Chivanhu theology is clear but in Christian theology these two very different types of beings have been conflated into one thing just as one clear example. This may seem like splitting hairs but for those who are experiencing the reality of that life knowing the difference can quite literally be a matter of life and death.

Blind speculation and superstition in the name of revelation has left many Zimbabweans ostracised in a society that seems to have developed a sort of "collective amnesia" concerning their own identity.

It is a national Stockholm's syndrome that sees black African Zimbabweans actually laughing at people who practice Chivanhu as if this sacred religion was a ridiculous made up manifestation of their own idle imaginations. We are in need of sober, honest and often difficult conversations around the concepts of deity that we hold onto and what the implications are for ourselves, our families, our loved ones and society at large.

As human beings we are in an ongoing negotiation with the idea of God. As our understanding and access to information has grown so too have our ideas of God. Religion has always evolved in this way and particularly Christianity has transformed with the times from society to society.

In Zimbabwe there has emerged a uniquely African perspective of Christ through the lens of AICs. Within many of these Churches are sincere saints seeking God with all honesty, sincerity and godly conviction in the name of Jesus. While there is widespread corruption, the issue of corruption is a human problem as corruption is not only in Churches but across all institutions wherever there are people you will find corruption, and that is just something we have to endure and look past if we are to find meaning.

The Christian And Chivanhu Concepts Of Good And Evil

The Christian Bible teaches that good and evil are opposing forces in the world. Good is often associated with God and righteousness, while evil is associated with the devil and sin. The concept of good and evil in Chivanhu is also based on the idea of opposing forces, with good being associated with the creator god Mwari and evil being associated with malevolent spirits.

In the Christian Bible, good is often described as actions that align with God's will and commandments. For example, in Matthew 22:37-39, Jesus says, "Love the Lord your God with all your heart and with all your soul and with all your mind. This is the first and greatest commandment. And the second is like it: 'Love your neighbor as yourself.'" These teachings emphasize the importance of love, compassion, and obedience to God.

Similarly, in Chivanhu, good is often associated with actions that align with Mwari's will and purpose for creation. The Chivanhu concept of good is often connected to the idea of "hunhu," which emphasizes the importance of treating others with kindness, respect, and empathy.

The Christian Bible also teaches that evil is often associated with the devil, also known as Satan. Satan is portrayed as a fallen angel who rebelled against God and seeks to tempt and deceive humans into sinning. In contrast, Chivanhu does not have a single figure like Satan, but instead recognizes the existence of malevolent spirits that can cause harm and misfortune to humans.

It is important to note that Mwari Musikavanhu is not considered to be Satan in Chivanhu. Mwari is the creator god who is responsible for the wellbeing of all of creation, including humans. The concept of Satan as a malevolent force opposing God is not present in Chivanhu theology.

Regarding the lack of prophecy in the Bible pointing to Zimbabwe, it is important to remember that the Bible was written in a specific historical context and primarily speaks to the experiences of the people and cultures in the Middle East. However, this does not mean that God is not present or active in other parts of the world, including Zimbabwe and other African nations.

The Argument Made By Jesus

One may be surprised to learn that people who have been initiated into Satanism are finding deliverance in Chivanhu with many testimonies of this nature on YouTube. Gogo Chihoro for example is a registered spirit medium who deals with such cases. People are being healed and delivered in the name of Mwari and his ancestral saints by the power of the Holy Spirit. Is this evidence of anything? Well Jesus Himself used this very argument:

Mark 3:22-30
And the scribes which came down from Jerusalem said, He hath Beelzebub, and by the prince of the devils casteth he out devils.
And he called them unto him, and said unto them in parables, How can Satan cast out Satan? And if a kingdom be divided against itself, that kingdom cannot stand. And if a house be divided against itself, that house cannot stand. And if Satan rise up against himself, and be divided, he cannot stand, but hath an end.
No man can enter into a strong man's house, and spoil his goods, except he will first bind the strong man; and then he will spoil his house.
Verily I say unto you, All sins shall be forgiven unto the sons of men, and blasphemies wherewith soever they shall blaspheme: But he that shall blaspheme against the Holy Ghost hath never forgiveness, but is in danger of eternal damnation: Because they said, He hath an unclean spirit.

Under sound Christian theology Satan cannot cast out Satan, in the words of Jesus Himself. Why then do we see Satanists being delivered in Chivanhu? It is because Chivanhu is not a religion of Satan is belongs to Mwari.

Chivanhu in fact does not prohibit its practitioners from going to Church but encourages as vadzimu are closest to those who live the kind of holy life Christianity encourages. Whatever Mwari is, he loves righteousness and holiness. Those who practice pure Chivanhu know this and many svikiro attend Church because the presence of the Holy Spirit is there and they are uplifted by Christian teachings of righteousness.

This is happening unofficially whether we like it or not. Many Church pastors practice Chivanhu privately because it works but they prohibit the Church because they love the praise of human beings more than the praise of God. This happens across all types of Churches from Catholic, Protestant to AICs. Some issues that require Chivanhu just fester for decades and in some cases people just die in a state of bondage because we have attempted to use Christianity in a place where Chivanhu would have been more effective.

The elephant in the room is that, officially the Holy Scriptures do not seem to allow for the practice of Chivanhu. Yet, Chivanhu did not exist when the entire Bible was written. At least, Zimbabwe and the Shona language itself did not exist just 2000 years ago. Somewhere within the past 1000 years when the major Bantu migrations happened and the various Shona dialects and Chivanhu religions evolved. It was a collective effort by various spiritual men and women across many generations.

Colonialism has only been a part of our story for the past 130 years. Are we really to believe that all our ancestors before the brutal colonisation of our people took place alongside the missionary work that converted our people by means of psychological manipulation and physical force, all of those people that existed before that were blindly serving Satan and are now in Hell? If God is a God of love and reason this just does not seem intellectually or emotionally sound for a God with infinite wisdom, love, intelligence and infinite resources.

One of the things which has happened is that, the Chivanhu religion was not written down and preserved in the form of scriptures. Chivanhu is transmitted by oral tradition but also by the spontaneous initiation from birth of various types of mediums. These mediums exist regardless of the preaching of the gospel, whether they pray in tongues and quote the Bible scriptures with deep conviction.

It is of absolutely no consequence to Mudzimu whether you are a "strong Christian" or not. Kusvikirwa does not come about because of a lack of faith. In fact the surprising part of it is that the only thing that seems to delay or hamper kusvikirwa is witchcraft. Those who practice witchcraft will frequently be hold positions in Church and advocate strongly against the practice of Chivanhu in the name of Christianity.

What is really it play is that such people know that within Chivanhu prophecy tends to be much deeper and better at solving issues of deep witchcraft. It was just given in this way by Mwari. Evil people are the loudest voices against Chivanhu and they do it using Christianity as an excuse to prevent people around them from getting relevant information from Chivanhu.

The Role of Spiritual Gifts in AIC

The Apostles in African initiated churches in Zimbabwe are known for moving in a remarkably similar way to the early Christian Apostles in terms of spiritual gifts. These spiritual gifts include healing, casting out demons, prophecy, miracles, signs, and wonders. These spiritual gifts are viewed as being given by the Holy Spirit to believers in order to edify the church and advance the gospel of Jesus Christ.

In these churches, spiritual gifts play a significant role in the life of the church. The spiritual gifts are seen as a manifestation of the Holy Spirit's presence and power in the church and are used to build up, encourage, and strengthen believers. They are also seen as a means of evangelism, as the power of God demonstrated through spiritual gifts can be a powerful witness to non-believers.

The importance of spiritual gifts in these churches lies in their ability to demonstrate the reality of God's power and presence. When people witness the power of God at work through the gifts of the Spirit, they are often drawn to the gospel and are more likely to believe. Additionally, spiritual gifts serve to build up and encourage believers, providing them with the strength and power they need to live out their faith in a world that is often hostile to Christianity.

There are several advantages to spreading the gospel through the power of the Holy Spirit and the use of spiritual gifts. First, it demonstrates the reality of God's power and presence, making the gospel more compelling and attractive to those who witness it. Second, it provides believers with the strength and power they need to live out their faith in a world that is often hostile to Christianity. Finally, it serves as a powerful witness to non-believers, drawing them to the gospel and leading them to faith in Jesus Christ.

In summary, the Apostles in African initiated churches in Zimbabwe move in a remarkably similar way to the early Christian Apostles in terms of spiritual gifts. These gifts play a significant role in the life of the church, providing believers with the strength and power they need to live out their faith and serving as a powerful witness to non-believers. Through the power of the Holy Spirit and the use of spiritual gifts, the gospel of Jesus Christ is advanced and lives are transformed.

The Concept of Mashavi in Chivanhu

Chivanhu is a traditional religion practiced by the Shona people of Zimbabwe. It is a religion that is deeply rooted in the belief in a supreme being, Mwari, who is the creator of all things. The Shona people believe that Mwari created the world and all that is in it, including the spirits and ancestors that inhabit it. The spirits and ancestors play an important role in the Chivanhu religion, and they are believed to be the intermediaries between humans and Mwari.

One of the key concepts in Chivanhu is the concept of mashavi. Mashavi are spirits that are believed to inhabit the natural world. They are often associated with specific places, such as rivers, mountains, and trees. The Shona people believe that mashavi have the power to influence human affairs, and they are often consulted for guidance and assistance.

There are many different types of mashavi, each with its own unique characteristics and powers. Mudzimu will often work closely with different types of mashavi in a person's life. They will draw the appropriate kind of shavi into a person's life in order to bring certain types of gifting into their life.

Not all mashavi are good, some are indeed evil. Mudzimu being good and holy will only draw mashavi which are good and holy into a person's life. According to Chivanhu theology, it is the madzinza spirits that draw mashavi that are evil into a person's life.

These evil mashavi are the ones that manifest during deliverance sessions even at Christian pentacostal church services. Only evil spirits will manifest during a deliverance service where the anointing of Jesus Christ is present deliver people from evil. Hence over time if your only exposure to mashavi comes from these type of deliverance services you may be forgiven for mistakenly thinking that mashavi are evil. This simply is not so.

Madzinza, which are spirits of the dead who walked in evil and not in the holy ways of Mwari Musikavanhu, work with evil mashavi.

Madzinza are like an evil type of mudzimu and they at times will even mimick mudzimu when they are being cast out. This again creates the confusion in people that mudzimu are evil spirits. This is not so, it takes one who is trained in Chivanhu working with Mudzimu to a high degree who is walking in a level of holiness to distinguish between good and evil mashavi, between Mudzimu and madzinza.

Guess work and interviewing dishonest evil spirits for information has really muddied the waters of revelation and truth in this area. One can distinguish between spirits through the Christian gift of discerning of spirits, yet without expert training what to do about what you see may still be just out of reach. When dealing with the issue of evil mashavi, a svikiro who has a good reputation of walking in holiness and helping their community has better grasp of what is happening and solutions for deliverance cases that seem difficult in a church set up are often routine and fairly simple in Chivanhu circles.

And of course for establishing good and holy mashavi, the only available option is Chivanhu. No other spiritual system is designed specifically to develop that aspect of spiritual gifting. Without expert guidance these gifts may lie dormant for years or even be the source of many spiritual attacks and attacks on one's health. The reason this happens is that varoyi (those practicing witchcraft) will seek to steal, intefer with or block (kutsipika) these mashavi from working in your life. If it is an area that you have not developed at all, you will be more vulnerable to attack and hence instead of bringing blessings to your life it can bring profound misfortune due to one's ignorance.

It will take another book to go into more detail about these things but for now I will just mention four types of mashavi briefly. All of these are holy and good when working with mudzimu and in the right context.

1. Mhondoro: Mhondoro is a type of mashavi that is associated with royalty and leadership. It is believed that the mhondoro spirit inhabits certain animals, such as lions, elephants, and leopards. The Shona people

believe that the mhondoro spirit can bestow power, protection, and good fortune upon those who are deemed worthy.

2. Manjuzu: Manjuzu are a manifestation of mashavi that are found all over the world and are called mermaids in English. In recent years manjuzu have attracted more notoriety and association with evil occultism than possitive affirmative publicity.

To begin, manjuzu can be good or evil. They are not all on one side with one agenda. Just as in the Christian Bible we have angels and fallen angels it is the same with mermaids. One should not seek after mermaids without first being strongly established in their own mudzimu or there is a risk of bringing an evil spirit into one's life.

Those who have manjuzu are normally like that from birth as mudzimu draws this shavi when a person is born. The manjuzu that are drawn by Mudzimu are automatically good and holy. Yet, many people that have this gifting do not practice Chivanhu at all and thus they become succeptible to evil spirits known in Shona as *Mbereka* these mbereka are called marine spirits in English and they are all evil. Manjuzu are not a type of marine spirit even though the dwell in water as mbereka do.

I can understand why some would believe that all spirits which are in water are evil marine spirits but this speculation while easy is not accurate. Marine spirits are actually enemies to mermaids and they are different types of spiritual beings altogether. Marine spirits are those beings that become spiritual husbands and spiritual wives that actually block and harass the manjuzu leading to misfortune and constant health problems.

Those with insufficient revelation and understanding concerning this will often blindly try to "cast out" the manjuzu as evil spirits. This does not work in the long term and even those short term results are not because the process was effective. It is just that mbereka get affected as a side effect of these deliverance sessions but even then they are not fully cast out.

People have been taught that any dreams or visions that take place under water originate from evil spirits. To put this into perspective it would be like saying all spirits that come from the air are good angels. This is not so. Fallen angels too are found in the air along with spiritual wickedness in "high places" (Ephesians 6:12). Likewise in the water there are evil spirits and there are also holy saintly spirits connected to God. There is no biblical basis to believe that only evil spirits can emerge out of water but at some point we see the mighty prophet Ezekiel swimming in water (Ezekiel 47:5). Not all visions or dreams in water need to lead us to panick as long as we are connected to the Holy Spirit. It is when we lack confidence in our own connection that finding someone who is well connected becomes necessary. The relevant knowledge about this is found almost entirely within Chivanhu by the Spirit of God.

Manjuzu is a type of shavi that is associated with fertility and childbirth. It is believed that the manjuzu spirit inhabits certain trees, such as the msasa tree. The Shona people believe that the manjuzu spirit can help women conceive and give birth to healthy children.

3. Ngirozi: Ngirozi is a type of mashavi that is associated with the afterlife. It is believed that the ngirozi spirit is the intermediary between the living and the dead. The Shona people believe that the ngirozi spirit can help guide the souls of the deceased to the afterlife. Ngirozi are also believed to bring a manifestation of the voice of Mwari Musikavanhu as they are close to God and to His Holy Spirit.

4. Ushavi hwema hombarume: This type of shavi is believed to bring wealth, fortune and good favour to those upon whom it is bestowed. It is this type of shavi that requires a person to have a type of cloth known as "jira reretso".

Understanding mashavi is essential to understanding Chivanhu cosmology. The Shona people believe that the natural world is inhabited by a multitude of spirits, each with its own unique characteristics and powers. These spirits are believed to be the intermediaries between humans and Mwari. By understanding the nature of these spirits and their relationship with Mwari, the Shona people are able to navigate their way through the challenges of life and seek the guidance and assistance they need.

Advantages Of Practicing Chivanhu

Having given a broad overview of few key issues that needed to be addressed, it seems good to finish with few points that briefly fill out the general idea of what Chivanhu is and what it seeks to accomplish. I will not go in-depth here as I do not wish to take attention away from the maim points, nevertheless these things are worth being aware of in our overall discourse on Zimbabwean Spirituality. Some advantages of Chivanhu are:

1. Cultural preservation: Chivanhu is an important aspect of Zimbabwean culture and practicing it can help preserve and maintain the country's cultural heritage.

2. Sense of community: Chivanhu emphasizes the importance of community and encourages individuals to work together for the greater good. This can foster a sense of belonging and connection among practitioners.

3. Spiritual guidance: Chivanhu provides a framework for understanding the spiritual world and offers guidance for navigating life's challenges.

4. Respect for nature: Chivanhu emphasizes the interconnectedness of all living things and encourages practitioners to respect and care for the natural world.

5. Ancestral connection: Chivanhu recognizes the importance of ancestral spirits and encourages practitioners to honor and connect with their ancestors.

6. Moral guidance: Chivanhu emphasizes the importance of living a moral and ethical life, which can provide a sense of purpose and direction.

7. Healing and wellness: Chivanhu includes practices such as herbal medicine, meditation, and ritual, which can promote physical, emotional, and spiritual healing and wellness.

8. Sense of identity: Practicing Chivanhu can help individuals connect with their Zimbabwean identity and heritage.

9. Reconciliation and forgiveness: Chivanhu emphasizes the importance of reconciliation and forgiveness, which can be beneficial for individuals and communities who have experienced conflict or trauma.

10. Empowerment: Chivanhu encourages individuals to take responsibility for their own lives and to work towards their goals and aspirations, which can foster a sense of empowerment and agency.

Contributions Chivanhu Can Make To The Global Community

Chivanhu, as a unique spiritual and cultural tradition, has the potential to make significant contributions to the world and the global community. Here are ten contributions that Chivanhu can make from both a metaphysical and practical perspective:

1. Promoting environmental awareness: Chivanhu emphasizes the interconnectedness of all living things, and encourages practitioners to respect and care for the natural world. This can contribute to a greater awareness and understanding of environmental issues, and promote sustainable practices.

2. Encouraging social justice: Chivanhu emphasizes the importance of community and working together for the greater good. This can contribute to a greater awareness of social justice issues, and encourage individuals and communities to work towards greater equality and fairness.

3. Fostering intercultural dialogue: Chivanhu is a deeply rooted Zimbabwean tradition, but it also has elements that can be shared and appreciated by people from other cultures. By promoting intercultural dialogue and understanding, Chivanhu can contribute to greater global harmony and appreciation of diversity.

4. Promoting holistic wellness: Chivanhu includes practices such as herbal medicine, meditation, and ritual, which can promote physical, emotional, and spiritual healing and wellness. By promoting holistic wellness, Chivanhu can contribute to greater overall health and wellbeing.

5. Encouraging personal responsibility: Chivanhu encourages individuals to take responsibility for their own lives and to work towards

their goals and aspirations. This can contribute to a greater sense of personal agency and empowerment.

6. Promoting forgiveness and reconciliation: Chivanhu emphasizes the importance of forgiveness and reconciliation, which can be beneficial for individuals and communities who have experienced conflict or trauma. By promoting forgiveness and reconciliation, Chivanhu can contribute to greater overall peace and harmony.

7. Encouraging ethical behavior: Chivanhu emphasizes the importance of living a moral and ethical life, which can contribute to greater overall ethical behavior in society.

8. Fostering spiritual growth: Chivanhu provides a framework for understanding the spiritual world and offers guidance for navigating life's challenges. By fostering spiritual growth, Chivanhu can contribute to greater overall personal and collective growth.

9. Encouraging cultural exchange: Chivanhu can be shared and appreciated by people from other cultures, and can contribute to greater cross-cultural exchange and understanding.

10. Promoting a sense of community: Chivanhu emphasizes the importance of community and working together for the greater good. By promoting a sense of community, Chivanhu can contribute to greater overal social cohesion and connectedness.

Conclusion

The fact that Chivanhu and Christianity coexist in Zimbabwe is not theoretical but it is a practical living reality whether we understand and accept it or not. Our permission in this divine matter is not required. What we do witness in many cases is a sort of hybrid religion where both systems can and do work together in various ways. This is a divine mystery which it is our great privilege and honour to witness.

In my personal experience and that of many people that attend and have founded AIC, the same Holy Spirit who speaks and guides people in the name of Jesus Christ in Christianity is the same Holy Spirit that is present speaking and guiding the saints in Chivanhu. A failure to grasp this reality is something that no one else of another race or nationality can do anything at all about in terms of intervening for us with easy ready made answers. Prayerful, meditative consideration is key for those of us who are the called according to God's purpose for this task.

It is only fear that silences the many voices who have seen and experienced this spiritual reality for themselves. To speak of spirituality in Zimbabwe is necessarily to speak of Christianity which is the most popular religion. Chivanhu practioners being in the minority actually face social persecution in Zimbabwe for practicing an indigenous religion. There is something unnatural and even unfortunate about that as to reject our own concepts of divinity in favour of another without the necessary due diligence is to betray ourselves in way that is difficult to put into words.

It is not for nothing that Christianity is a mighty spiritual force in Zimbabwe. The divine Biblical scriptures place a heavy emphasis on righteousness and holiness which is the universal language of spirituality. Righteousness is simply a practical way to live life regardless of one's religion and ethnicity. For this we bow at the divinity of Christ Jesus whose message of divine love and reconciliation to God is a pillar for all humanity whereby salvation has come to all those who accept Him.

This same righteousness is required in the practice of Chivanhu and by itself righteousness living can a does deliver a person from much evil. We do not have to take anything away from Christianity concerning this and it is an expression of divinity that is sufficient for most people. Those who are having an excellent experience with Christianity need not add anything at all to that, it is a holy and perfect way to relate to God as it is and if it was not already clear, I personally love Jesus and Christianity.

What is clear to me is that there remains a percentage of people for which Chivanhu remains the only viable option in terms of spiritual realisation with God. That is just the way it is for some peope. Love Jesus or not, for some people the circumstance of their spiritual lives do not permit them to not practice Chivanhu without experiencing dire consequences. A crisis of conscience will haunt these ones if they are strong Christians as indeed it haunted me.

It is the grace of God that appeared to me and taught me there is in fact one God but different ways to view Him. The Chivanhu view of God is righteous and holy view when it is practiced with the appropriate knowledge and guidance. This knowledge and guidance must be transmitted by human beings as indeed all religions including Christianity are transmitted by human beings. There is sacred noble honour that comes with standing up bearing the tremendous weight of this awesome responsibilty. It is when Chivanhu is practiced with this level of clarity and conviction that God the Holy Spirit shows up in the most sublime ways. To put it more succintly, God respond to unwavering faith that is free from doubt and He rewards this faith by the manifestation of His power, glory and presence.

To those who are called on the holy path of Chivanhu, you do not have to apologise for it but rather, celebrate the fact that God has counted you worthy to be part of the spiritual force that restores the strong spiritual foundations of Zimbabwe. Our ancient ancestors were shot in the back and hung whilst dead before they were beheaded and their sacred bones were shipped to England where they remain till very day in 2023. Those who committed these atrocities are long dead but the negative energy of the fear they put into a society that had to witness their Heros being brutally murdered remains with us as a collective generational curse of the fear of Chivanhu. Fear is not a spirit that comes from God. If light must come we must learn to recognise fear and intolerance and barbaric tools that are not worthy of all those that call on the name of Jesus in sincerity.

Jesus spoke a parable of "the good Samaritan". Samaritans practiced a religion that would be considered worse than Chivanhu in terms of its idea of who God is. Despite this Jesus paradoxically speaks of a "good" Samaritan. In this Jesus was saying that is not the name of the religion and the titles that we carry that make us spiritual however it is our very attitudes towards one another. How do we treat someone whom we do not perceive any spiritual benefit from? The Samaritan had nothing to gain from helping the theologically different Jew. It was pure compassion and love that actually showed his spiritual prowess. It is my prayer that we should adopt this attitude of tolerance and compassion one towards another.

Our ancestral saints in Zimbabwe represent a kind of spiritual intimacy and mentorship that is intensely sacred. Mudzimu has great love for the people who it visits. When you perceive this love, your ability to connect with your Mudzimu is greatly multiplied. You will receive divine guidance in a way that is distinctly different from the working of angels and even the working of saints of another religion. These ancestral saints represent those who faced similar trials as you in their past but they overcame those trials and their strength and wisdom is present not only spiritually but it is in your very life's blood.

I have covered much ground here in general terms so as to give snapshot of my views. By the grace of Mwari Musikavanhu and the Lord Jesus Christ more books will follow that look at individual topics in more detail. Amen.

References

1. Mbiti, John. "Concept of God in Africa." Journal of Black Theology in South Africa, vol. 1, no. 1, 1987, pp. 3-15.

2. Ndagurwa, Hilton. "Mwari and the Shona: A Study of the Concept of Deity among the Shona." Journal of Theology for Southern Africa, vol. 48, 1984, pp. 3-14.

3. Ranger, Terence. "The Invention of Tradition Revisited: The Case of Zimbabwe." Journal of Southern African Studies, vol. 15, no. 1, 1989, pp. 39-61.

4. Shoko, Tabona. "Mwari: God of the Shona People of Zimbabwe." Journal of Religion in Africa, vol. 37, no. 2, 2007, pp. 261-284.

5. Zvobgo, Chengetai J. "The Relevance of Traditional Religion in the Modern World: A Study of the Shona Religion in Zimbabwe." Journal of Black Studies, vol. 37, no. 6, 2007, pp. 941-957.

6. Chitando, Ezra. "The Place of Ancestral Religion in Zimbabwe Today: A Critique of Some Recent Developments." Journal of Theology for Southern Africa, vol. 115, 2003, pp. 3-20.

7. Dube, Musa W. "The Concept of God in African Traditional Religion: A Critical Analysis." Missionalia, vol. 24, no. 1, 1996, pp. 5-20.

8. Gelfand, Michael. "Shona Religion." Rhodes-Livingstone Journal, vol. 21, no. 1, 1954, pp. 1-14.

9. Hodza, A. F. "Mwari Cult in Zimbabwe." African Studies, vol. 8, no. 2, 1949, pp. 77-80.

10. Kawinga, Lukas S. "The Concept of God in African Traditional Religion: A Philosophical Reflection." Journal of Theology for Southern Africa, vol. 142, 2012, pp. 3-15.

11. Kusmierz, Katrin. "The Concept of God in African Traditional Religion." Religions, vol. 5, no. 4, 2014, pp. 961-975.

12. Magesa, Laurenti. "The Concept of God in African Traditional Religion." Journal of Theology for Southern Africa, vol. 51, 1985, pp. 3-15.

13. Makuvaza, M. "The Concept of God in African Traditional Religion: A Zimbabwean Perspective." International Journal of Humanities and Social Science Research, vol. 4, no. 1, 2014, pp. 58-67.

14. Chitando, Ezra. "The Dynamics of Christianization in Zimbabwe: An Overview." Studies in World Christianity, vol. 9, no. 1, 2003, pp. 75-98.

15. Gunda, Masiiwa Ragies. "The Impact of Christianity on African Culture." International Journal of Humanities and Social Science Research, vol. 1, no. 2, 2012, pp. 13-26.

16. Kamwendo, Gregory. "Chivanhu and Christianity: Towards a Syncretic Understanding." Journal of Religion in Africa, vol. 39, no. 3, 2009, pp. 297-318.

17. Kambarami, Masiiwa Ragies. "Chivanhu in the Context of Shona Religion." Zimbabwean Journal of Religious Studies, vol. 1, no. 1, 2016, pp. 1-15.

18. Kapinga, Frederick. "Christianity and African Traditional Religion: The Search for a Synthesis." Journal of Religion in Africa, vol. 26, no. 1, 1996, pp. 33-57.

19. Kaunda, James M. "The Shona Concept of Chivanhu and the Christian Doctrine of Creation." Journal of Theology for Southern Africa, vol. 107, 2000, pp. 67-80.

20. Kefa, Simeon. "The Missing Link: A Comparative Study of Christianity and African Traditional Religion." Journal of Religion and Theology, vol. 1, no. 1, 2015, pp. 1-11.

21. Machingura, Francisca. "The Shona Concept of Chivanhu and its Compatibility with Christianity." Journal of African Studies and Development, vol. 5, no. 3, 2013, pp. 70-78.

22. Madanhire, Ignatius. "The Significance of Chivanhu in the Context of Zimbabwean Christianity." African Journal of Religion and Philosophy, vol. 1, no. 1, 1996, pp. 45-55.

23. Makoni, Sinfree. "The Challenge of African Traditional Religion to Christian Theology." Journal of Theology for Southern Africa, vol. 123, 2005, pp. 72-83.

24. Mamiya, Lawrence A. "The Syncretism of African Traditional Religion and Christianity in Zimbabwe." The Journal of Religion in Africa, vol. 29, no. 3, 1999, pp. 298-325.

25. Mare, Gerrie. "The Use of the Shona Concept of Chivanhu in Interpreting the Bible." Journal of Theology for Southern Africa, vol. 116, 2003, pp. 74-81.

26. Mbiti, John S. "The Encounter of African Traditional Religion and Christianity." Journal of Theology for Southern Africa, vol. 39, 1982, pp. 2-11.

27. Mhute, Shepherd. "Chivanhu and Christianity: A Study of the Syncretism of Shona Traditional Religion and Christianity in Zimbabwe." International Journal of African Renaissance

28. Chakrabarti, A. (2017). The Universal Significance of Chivanhu Religion. International Journal of Humanities and Social Science Research, 5(2), 26-33.

29. Chigwedere, A. (2018). The Role of Chivanhu Religion in Zimbabwean Society. Journal of African Cultural Studies, 30(1), 82-94.

30. Chinamasa, P. (2017). The Resilience of Chivanhu Religion in Zimbabwe. Journal of Religion and Society, 19(1), 12-23.

31. Mafukidze, T. (2015). The Sacredness of Chivanhu Religion. Journal of African Religion and Philosophy, 1

32. The Holy Bible, English Standard Version. Crossway, 2016.

33. Nyamwanza, Taurai Emmanuel. "Mwari: A Belief in a High God in Zimbabwe." Journal of Pan African Studies, vol. 4, no. 4, 2011, pp. 115-128.

34. "Yahweh." Encyclopædia Britannica. Encyclopædia Britannica, Inc., n.d. Web. 15 May. 2023.

35. The Holy Bible, English Standard Version. Crossway, 2016.

36. "Qadosh." Theological Wordbook of the Old Testament, edited by R. Laird Harris, Moody Press, 1980, pp. 697-698.

37. "Hagios." Theological Dictionary of the New Testament, edited by Gerhard Kittel and Gerhard Friedrich, Eerdmans, 1964, pp. 17-23.

38. Chitando, Ezra. "Ancestral Spirits and Christianity in Zimbabwe: A Case Study of the United Methodist Church." Studia Historiae Ecclesiasticae, vol. XXXI, no. 2, 2005,

39. Chirisa, Innocent, and Josephine Nhongo-Simbanegavi. "Great Zimbabwe: An African empire." Journal of Southern African Studies 44, no. 4 (2018): 631-646.

40. Curtis, Matthew. "The archaeology of trade and exchange in southern Africa." Journal of Social Archaeology 10, no. 3 (2010): 378-400.

41. Pikirayi, Innocent. "The Zimbabwe Culture: Origins and Decline of Southern Zambezian States." Journal of African History 52, no. 1 (2011): 1-19.

Don't miss out!

Visit the website below and you can sign up to receive emails whenever Gabriel James Dziya publishes a new book. There's no charge and no obligation.

https://books2read.com/r/B-A-IQXT-FHEJC

Connecting independent readers to independent writers.

Also by Gabriel James Dziya

Anthology Of Heavenly Visions
Demystifying The Anointing
Prophecies And Their Testimonies
Mwari, Chivanhu & Christianity

www.ingramcontent.com/pod-product-compliance
Lightning Source LLC
Chambersburg PA
CBHW021753150726
47989CB00004B/1631